# Thinking Skills: (

## Table of Conte

# Thinking Skills: Grade 6

## Introduction

In today's world of tremendous technological changes, it is of utmost importance that students learn how to be critical and creative thinkers. Research shows that thinking-skills instruction enhances students' learning and increases their ability to reason. It is the aim of *Thinking Skills* to further aid these goals.

But how do teachers include another element in a curriculum that is already overloaded? This series was developed to meet the needs of a teacher's busy and crowded schedule by providing activity-based thinking lessons that

- build creative and critical thinking skills across the curriculum.
- can be easily incorporated into existing lesson plans.
- accommodate different learning styles.
- address both linear and higher-order thinking skills.
- involve both specific answer responses and open-ended problems to be solved.
- are standards-based.
- incorporate multiple levels of Bloom's taxonomy.
- are self-guided, allowing students to work without teacher assistance.
- give students opportunities to work individually, with partners, or in small groups.

**Organization**

This book provides a collection of 16 lessons that are grouped into four units. The units develop concepts taught at this grade level. Each lesson is based on a five-step activity that focuses on one key thinking skill.

Each lesson contains three types of pages:

- The first page is a calendar that guides students step by step through each lesson. These pages are intended to be self-directed. Due dates can be assigned and recorded on the calendar so students are aware of the deadlines. A materials list at the bottom of the page details additional resources or supplies teachers need to prepare in advance.
- The second page in the lesson introduces the key thinking skill. It offers an explanation and example of the skill, as well as follow-up questions. The last section guides students through an activity based on the skill.
- The final page in each lesson is Reflect. The questions on this page focus on the activity and encourage students to think metacognitively about how they used the key thinking skill. The Think Link section at the bottom of the page suggests an extension activity so students can further practice the skill and transfer the knowledge to other pertinent areas.

## Use

This book provides students with practice using thinking skills in conjunction with existing curriculum topics. Lessons can be chosen based on the topic or on a specific thinking skill. The table of contents and the skills matrix can help locate specific topics or thinking skills.

*Thinking Skills* offers flexibility in use. The lessons can be set up in a station or organized into individual packets. The station method requires less photocopying and organization, but requires room space. By using packets, students can work during their free time at school or complete the lessons as homework.

Determine the implementation that fits your students' needs and classroom structure. The following plan suggests one possible format.

### Step 1

Introduce the topic. Give a brief overview of the activity, what students will do daily, and how they are to complete the tasks. Assign the due dates and have students record the dates on their calendars. Allow students time to complete the work sheet that explains the key thinking skill.

### Steps 2–4

Students work on an extended activity for three days. At least one day in each lesson, students will use a graphic organizer to record their thoughts and to help them focus on the thinking process.

### Step 5

After students complete the Reflect activity sheet, gather students to share their completed activity and to discuss the thinking process.

## Additional Notes

1. Each daily activity should take no more than 25 minutes.
2. Students can complete the writing assignments on their own paper.
3. Many of the activities for Steps 2 through 4 are open-ended. Accept all reasonable answers as long as students can explain their reasoning.
4. Be sure to photocopy necessary pages, materials, and resources in advance to have them available to students. You may want to store them in a folder if students will be working in a station.

## Skills Matrix

A skills matrix can be found on page 4. It identifies the thinking skills and the subjects associated with each. A check mark (✔) identifies the key skill of each lesson, while an X (✘) notes additional skills that students practice during the course of the lesson.

## Resources

There are two kinds of resources included in *Thinking Skills*. Pages 53 through 60 include blank graphic organizers to help students organize their thoughts and facilitate the thinking process. Pages 61 through 63 are topic resource pages that accompany several of the lessons. The materials section at the bottom of each calendar page identifies the pages students will need. You will need to review the lessons in advance, as some activities ask that students have multiple copies of one graphic organizer.

# Skills Matrix

| Thinking Skill | Lesson | | | | | | | | | | | | | | | |
|---|---|---|---|---|---|---|---|---|---|---|---|---|---|---|---|---|
| | 1 | 2 | 3 | 4 | 5 | 6 | 7 | 8 | 9 | 10 | 11 | 12 | 13 | 14 | 15 | 16 |
| Classifying | | | | ✘ | ✔ | ✘ | | | | | ✘ | | | | | |
| Comparing and Contrasting | | | ✔ | ✘ | ✘ | | | | | ✘ | ✘ | | | | | |
| Creating Metaphors | | | | ✘ | | ✔ | | | | | | | | | | |
| Determining Cause and Effect | | | | | | | | ✘ | ✘ | | | ✔ | | | | ✘ |
| Determining Reliability of Sources | | | | | | | | | | | ✘ | | ✘ | ✔ | | |
| Finding Reasons and Conclusions | | | | | | ✘ | ✔ | | | | | | | | | |
| Generating Possibilities | ✘ | | | | ✘ | ✘ | ✘ | | ✘ | | | ✘ | ✘ | ✘ | ✔ | |
| Inferring | | | | ✘ | | | | ✔ | | | | ✘ | ✘ | | | |
| Making Decisions | | | ✘ | | ✘ | | | | ✘ | | ✔ | | | ✘ | | ✘ |
| Making Generalizations | ✘ | | | ✔ | | | | | | | | ✘ | | | | ✘ |
| Predicting | | | | | | | | ✘ | | | | | | | | ✔ |
| Reasoning by Analogy | | | | | | | | | | ✔ | | | | | | |
| Sequencing | | ✔ | | | | | | | ✘ | | | | | ✘ | ✘ | |
| Solving Problems | | | | | | | | | ✔ | | | ✘ | | | | |
| Uncovering Assumptions | | | | | | | | | | | | | ✔ | | | |
| Understanding Parts to Whole Relationships | ✔ | ✘ | ✘ | ✘ | | | | ✘ | ✘ | ✘ | | | | | | |
| **Curriculum Area** | | | | | | | | | | | | | | | | |
| Art/Music | | | | | | • | | | • | | • | | | • | | |
| Health | | | | | • | • | • | • | | | | • | | | • | |
| Language Arts | | • | | | | • | • | • | | • | | • | • | | | |
| Math | • | • | • | • | • | | | | | • | • | | • | • | • | • |
| Science | | | | | | | | | • | | | | • | | | |
| Social Studies | • | • | • | • | | | • | • | • | • | • | • | | • | | |

✔ = Key Skill ✘ = Additional Skill • = Curriculum Area

Name ______________________________ Date ______________

# Classroom Map

Lesson 1

Maps are drawings of real places. For example, your school has a map to show all the rooms in the school. People visiting the school can easily walk to a room if they have a map. But what might happen if part of the map is missing? You will explore the importance of each part of a map. Then you will draw a map of your classroom and all its features to scale.

## Step 1

Due Date: ______________________________

KEY SKILL

### Understanding Parts to Whole Relationships

Complete page 6.

## Step 2

Due Date: ______________________________

**Identify map parts.**

1. Get the Bend River Map.
2. Underline the title. Draw a box around the compass rose. Draw a star beside the distance scale. Circle the map key.
3. Take turns asking a partner questions about the map. You may want to ask questions that relate to the distance scale.
4. Discuss with a partner what would happen if each part of the map was missing.

## Step 3

Due Date: ______________________________

**Measure the classroom.**

1. Draw a two-column chart. Label the first column "Classroom Parts." Label the second column "Measurements."
2. With a partner, discuss the special parts and important features in the classroom. List each in the Classroom Parts column.
3. Using a tape measure or yardstick, measure the room, the parts of the room, and the important features you listed. Record each measurement in the Measurements column.

## Step 4

Due Date: ______________________________

**Draw a map.**

1. Get a sheet of Graph Paper. Look at the chart you made in Step 3.
2. Draw a map of the classroom. Make sure the classroom size, parts, and features are proportional to each other. Also, include all the parts of a map. Don't forget the compass rose.
3. Save the map for another lesson.

## Step 5

Due Date: ______________________________

REFLECT Complete page 7.

**Materials:** Bend River Map (Resources, p. 61), Graph Paper (Resources, p. 60), yardsticks, measuring tapes, map pencils

Name ______________________________ Date ________________

# KEY SKILL Understanding Parts to Whole Relationships

Everything can be broken into smaller **parts**, or pieces. It is important to look at each part to understand how it works. It is also important to look at how all the parts work together to make the **whole**. All the parts work together to form a **relationship**. Changing one part often changes how the parts work together.

**Example**

Fred was driving to a store. He missed a turn and got lost. He looked through his maps. He pulled out the map with the title "West River," the name of his town. The distance scale had been torn from the corner of the map. Fred was not sure how much farther he had to drive.

**Answer the questions.**

**1.** What parts are named in the example?

______________________________

**2.** When put together, what whole item do the parts make?

______________________________

**3.** How does one missing part change this item's use?

______________________________

______________________________

**For 4–6, follow the directions to find the parts of a classroom.**

**4.** Name four parts of a classroom.

______________________________

______________________________

**5.** Tell the use of each part.

______________________________

______________________________

**6.** Tell what would happen if these parts were not in a classroom.

______________________________

______________________________

Name ______________________ Date ____________

# REFLECT

**Answer the questions.**

**1.** What are three parts of your classroom? Tell why each part is important.

______________________________________________

______________________________________________

______________________________________________

**2.** How could you find out what would happen if a part were changed or missing?

______________________________________________

**3.** Circle one part you listed in question 1. What might happen if this part is missing?

______________________________________________

______________________________________________

**4.** How did thinking about the parts of a classroom help you draw a map?

______________________________________________

______________________________________________

**5.** Why is the distance scale important on a map?

______________________________________________

______________________________________________

**6.** How will thinking about parts help you understand other things?

______________________________________________

______________________________________________

## Think Link

Think about the different parts that make up your school. Make a list of eight different parts. Tell what might happen if each part is missing from the school campus.

Name ______________________ Date ______________

# Written Directions

Lesson 2

Following directions is an important skill, not only in school, but when doing outside activities. It is equally important to be able to give clear directions. You will practice writing and drawing directions on a map to guide a classmate to find something you hide. How good will your directions be?

## Step 1 Due Date: ______________

KEY SKILL

**Sequencing**

Complete page 9.

## Step 2 Due Date: ______________

**Draw and write directions.**

1. Hide a crayon someplace in the classroom, such as behind a book in a shelf. Be sure to choose a place where it can stay safely for several days. Write your name on a piece of tape and tape the crayon in place.
2. Get the map of the classroom you drew in Lesson 1. Draw a line from the door to the place the crayon is hidden.
3. Now you will write the directions. Get a Sequence Chart. Write a title.
4. What will someone need to find the crayon? Make a list of all the materials in the top oval on the chart.
5. Look at your map. In what direction will a person go to find the crayon? Is the crayon above or below something? Write one step in each box of the chart. Get another Sequence Chart if you need one.

## Step 3 Due Date: ______________

**Follow your directions.**

1. Follow the directions you wrote step by step. Did you find your crayon?
2. Correct the directions on your Sequence Chart if you need to.
3. Get another Sequence Chart. Rewrite the directions.

## Step 4 Due Date: ______________

**Trade written directions.**

1. Trade Sequence Charts with a classmate.
2. Follow the directions. Did you and your classmate give good directions? Together, discuss your findings.

## Step 5 Due Date: ______________

REFLECT Complete page 10.

**Materials:** crayon, tape, Lesson 1 classroom map, Sequence Chart (Resources, p. 53)

Name ______________________ Date ____________

# KEY SKILL Sequencing

**Sequence** is the order in which things happen. When you make or do something, you are following a sequence of steps. The steps have a special order.

**Example**
Angie decides to take her dog for a walk. She lives on Oak Drive and begins walking north one block. Then, Angie turns left on Park Street and walks west for two blocks. Next, she turns left on Knob Hill and walks southeast for four blocks. Finally, Angie and her dog are home.

**Answer the questions.**

1. What does Angie do in the example?

_______________________________________________

2. In which direction did Angie walk first?

_______________________________________________

3. In which direction did Angie walk on Knob Hill?

_______________________________________________

4. How many blocks did Angie walk in all?

_______________________________________________

**For 5–6, follow the directions to tell how to sharpen a pencil.**

5. Tell the materials you need.

_______________________________________________

6. Write at least three steps to tell how to sharpen a pencil.

_______________________________________________

_______________________________________________

_______________________________________________

Name ______________________ Date ______________

# REFLECT

**Answer the questions.**

**1.** Why is it important to tell how to do something in order?

________________________________________

________________________________________

**2.** Why is it important to list all the equipment needed to complete an activity?

________________________________________

________________________________________

**3.** How did using a Sequence Chart help you tell the directions?

________________________________________

________________________________________

**4.** Did you rewrite your directions after you looked for the crayon? If so, tell why.

________________________________________

________________________________________

**5.** Was it easier or harder to follow your directions or the directions of your classmate? Explain. ________________________________

________________________________________

**6.** How will thinking about sequence help you tell how to do or make other things?

________________________________________

________________________________________

## Think Link

Write directions to tell how to get from your classroom to the cafeteria. Include an estimate of the distance that someone would walk.

Name ______________________ Date ______________

# Landform Maps

Lesson 3

There are many kinds of maps. A landform map shows the shape of the land, like plains and mountains. A resource map shows the locations of resources, like trees and oil. You will examine two maps to tell how they are alike and different. Then, you will draw landforms on an imaginary country in which you would like to live.

## Step 1 Due Date: ______________

KEY SKILL

**Comparing and Contrasting**

Complete page 12.

## Step 2 Due Date: ______________

**Compare and contrast two maps.**

1. Get the Brazil Maps activity sheet.
2. Get a Venn Diagram. Write the name of each kind of map above one of the circles.
3. How are the maps alike? Write notes where the circles overlap.
4. How are the maps different? Write notes in the circle under each name.

## Step 3 Due Date: ______________

**Look at landforms.**

1. Look at the landform map of Brazil. What kinds of landforms do you see? How are these landforms shown?
2. Get the Map of Asouby activity sheet. Suppose you are going to live in this country. Think about the kinds of landforms the country should have and where they should be.
3. Make a landform map for the country of Asouby. Be sure to include all the parts of a map.

## Step 4 Due Date: ______________

**Compare and contrast landform maps.**

1. Work with a partner. Look at both maps of Asouby. Discuss the locations of the landforms and the reason each location was chosen.
2. Get a Venn Diagram. Complete the diagram to show how you and your partner's maps of Asouby are alike and different.
3. Is there anything you would like to change on your map? If so, draw a new landform map of Asouby.
4. Save the map for another lesson.

## Step 5 Due Date: ______________

REFLECT Complete page 13.

**Materials:** Brazil Maps (Resources, p. 61), Venn Diagram (Resources, p. 54), Map of Asouby (Resources, p. 62), map pencils

Name ______________________ Date ____________

# KEY SKILL Comparing and Contrasting

You **compare** to show how things are alike.
You **contrast** to show how things are different.

**Example**

Austin and Houston are large cities located in Texas. Houston is near the Gulf of Mexico in the southeastern part of the state. It is an important shipping city. Austin is in the center of the state. It is the capital of Texas.

**Answer the questions.**

1. What two places are being compared and contrasted in the example?

______________________________

2. How are these two places alike?

______________________________

3. How are these two places different?

______________________________

______________________________

**For 4–6, follow the directions to compare and contrast two cities in your state.**

4. Name two cities in your state. ______________________________

5. Name three ways these cities are alike.

______________________________

______________________________

______________________________

6. Name three ways these cities are different.

______________________________

______________________________

______________________________

Name ______________________ Date ____________

# REFLECT

**Answer the questions.**

**1.** What did you learn about the maps after comparing and contrasting them?

______________________________________________

______________________________________________

**2.** When comparing and contrasting the maps, what did you find important?

______________________________________________

**3.** How did using the Venn Diagram help you think?

______________________________________________

______________________________________________

**4.** How can comparing and contrasting help you make choices?

______________________________________________

______________________________________________

**5.** Would you use this way of thinking again if you had to make choices? Explain.

______________________________________________

______________________________________________

## Think Link

Suppose your family wants to take a vacation. One family member wants to go to the mountains. Another wants to go to the beach. Compare and contrast both places and choose the one you would vote to visit.

Name ______________________ Date ______________

# Landforms and Resources

Lesson 4

The landforms of a place often give clues about the kinds of resources found in an area. You will examine the kinds of resources common to specific landforms and make generalizations about their relationship. Then, you will add resources to the landform map of the imaginary country of Asouby.

## Step 1

Due Date: ______________

KEY SKILL

### Making Generalizations

Complete page 15.

## Step 2

Due Date: ______________

**Make generalizations.**

1. Get the Brazil Maps activity sheet. Get a Matrix Chart.
2. Write the names of the landforms in the boxes across the top. These are "Landforms to Compare."
3. Write the names of the resources in the boxes along the left side of the chart.
4. Fill in the Matrix Chart. Write a plus sign (+) in the box to show if the resource can be found in this landform. Put a minus sign (–) in the box if it cannot. Put an X in the box if you cannot tell from the map.
5. Make five generalizations about the relationship of a resource and where it is found. For example: Minerals are an important resource in mountains.

## Step 3

Due Date: ______________

**Explore if the generalizations are true.**

1. Look at your Matrix Chart and the generalizations you made in Step 2.
2. Check your generalizations by studying landform and resource maps of other places to get a bigger sample.
3. Are your generalizations true? Discuss with a partner why or why not. Make new generalizations if you need to.

## Step 4

Due Date: ______________

**Complete a map.**

1. Get the landform map of Asouby you drew in Lesson 3.
2. Draw symbols to show resources on the map. Include another key to show what the symbols represent.

## Step 5

Due Date: ______________

REFLECT Complete page 16.

**Materials:** Brazil Maps (Resources, p. 61), Matrix Chart (Resources, p. 55), landform and resource maps, Lesson 3 Asouby landform map

Name ______________________________ Date ________________

# KEY SKILL Making Generalizations

A **generalization** is something people believe to be true about all the things in a group. It is important to be careful when making generalizations. They may not be true. A **sample** can help show if a generalization is true. A sample tests a small part of a big group to see if the belief is true.

**Example**

Anna and her family live along the coast of Maine. The family owns a boat and earns a living by fishing. When Anna's family went on a vacation to Florida, Anna found the people along the coast also fished. She wondered if people living on the west coast fished, too. She read a book and discovered that fishing along the Pacific Ocean is an important industry.

**Answer the questions.**

**1.** By what landform did Anna live?

______________________________

**2.** What resource did Anna's family use?

______________________________

**3.** How did Anna's family use this resource? ______________________________

______________________________

**4.** Based on the information Anna learned in the example, what generalizations can she make?

______________________________

**For 5–6, follow the directions to make a generalization.**

**5.** Look at the Brazil maps. Tell where most of Brazil's cities are located.

______________________________

______________________________

**6.** Make a generalization about where people build cities.

______________________________

Name ______________________ Date ____________

# REFLECT

**Answer the questions.**

**1.** What were two generalizations you made about landforms and resources?

______________________________________________

______________________________________________

**2.** Do you think the sample was big enough? Explain.

______________________________________________

______________________________________________

**3.** Would your generalizations change if the sample got bigger? Explain.

______________________________________________

______________________________________________

**4.** Why do you think it is important to have a big sample to find out if a generalization is true?

______________________________________________

______________________________________________

**5.** What might happen if you made a generalization without taking a sample?

______________________________________________

______________________________________________

## Think Link

Think about the places in the community you visit. Is there a place you visit more than the others? Are there several places you like to go? If so, do these places have something in common? Make a generalization about the places you like to visit.

Name ______________________ Date ______________

# Sport Sort

Lesson 5

There are many kinds of sports. Some sports involve balls, some involve running, and some involve both. You and a partner will make a list of different sports and find two different ways to sort them.

## Step 1 Due Date: ______________

KEY SKILL

**Classifying**

Complete page 18.

## Step 2 Due Date: ______________

**List kinds of sports.**

1. Work with a partner to brainstorm a list of 20 different sports.
2. Cut paper into rectangles to make 20 cards.
3. Write the name of each sport you listed on a card. On the back, write important details about the sport, such as the equipment used, number of players on a team, how players move, or where the sport is played.

## Step 3 Due Date: ______________

**Classify the sports.**

1. With your partner, find a way to classify the sports. Use the cards to help order the groups. Think of a label for each group. All of the sports may not be needed.
2. Get a Concept Web. Write "Sports" in the Topic box.
3. Record the group labels in the large ovals. Add more ovals if needed.
4. Write the name of each sport in a small oval. Draw more small ovals if needed.

## Step 4 Due Date: ______________

**Classify the sports a different way.**

1. Look at the way you and your partner classified the sports in Step 3. With your partner, find a second way to classify the sports. Use the cards to help order the groups again. Think of a label for each group.
2. Get another Concept Web. Write "Sports" in the Topic box.
3. Record the group labels and sport names in the ovals as before.
4. Look at both Concept Webs. Choose the best way to classify the sports.
5. Share your groupings with the class.

## Step 5 Due Date: ______________

REFLECT Complete page 19.

**Materials:** construction paper, scissors, Concept Web (Resources, p. 56)

Name ______________________ Date ____________

# KEY SKILL Classifying

**Classifying** is a way to group things according to how they are alike. The group will have a trait, or characteristic, that is the same. Classifying helps tell what something is.

**Example**

Think about balls used in different games. How can they be grouped?

**A.** Trait: ball size
Large: soccer, football, volleyball
Small: baseball, table tennis, golf ball

**B.** Trait: how the ball is moved
Kicked: soccer, football
Hit: volleyball, baseball, table tennis, golf ball

**Answer the questions.**

**1.** What trait is used to group balls in Example A?

______________________________

**2.** What trait is used to group balls in Example B?

______________________________

**For 3–5, follow the directions to classify clothing.**

**3.** Make a list of six items of clothing.

______________________________

______________________________

**4.** Classify the clothing items by where they are worn.

______________________________

______________________________

**5.** Classify the clothing items by what they are made of.

______________________________

______________________________

Name ______________________ Date ______________

# REFLECT

**Answer the questions.**

**1.** What did you think about when you classified sports in two different ways?

______________________________________________

______________________________________________

**2.** What helped you decide which was the best way to classify the sports?

______________________________________________

______________________________________________

**3.** How did using a Concept Web help you classify the sports?

______________________________________________

______________________________________________

**4.** What is the reason that people classify things?

______________________________________________

______________________________________________

**5.** How will classifying help you to think about ways that other things can be grouped?

______________________________________________

______________________________________________

## Think Link

Look in your desk. Find the best way to classify the items in it.

Name ______________________ Date ______________

# Team Mascot

Lesson 6

Suppose some coaches have asked you to join a new team they are forming. The players on the team will choose the team name and mascot. A mascot is an animal, person, or thing that represents a group. What team mascot will you suggest?

## Step 1

Due Date: ______________________

KEY SKILL

### Creating Metaphors

Complete page 21.

## Step 2

Due Date: ______________________

### Choose a mascot.

1. Choose a favorite sport.
2. Get a Concept Web. Write the name of the sport in the Topic box.
3. Think about the important skills that team members should have to play the sport. Include not only game skills, but skills for being a good sport, too. Record these skills in the large ovals. Add more ovals if needed.
4. Think of animals, people, or things that have the same traits as the skills in the large ovals. Write in the small ovals two suggestions for each characteristic. You might write the same name for different traits.
5. Look at your web. Which mascot could best represent the team? Circle it.

## Step 3

Due Date: ______________________

### Make a team T-shirt.

1. Get a sheet of paper. Draw two T-shirt outlines.
2. Create a front and back T-shirt design showing the mascot you chose for the team. You may wish to include a slogan.

## Step 4

Due Date: ______________________

### Write a letter.

1. Write a short letter to the coaches telling them about your mascot choice. Use ideas from your web about important sport skills to explain why your mascot choice should be chosen.
2. Display the letter with your drawing.

## Step 5

Due Date: ______________________

REFLECT Complete page 22.

**Materials:** Concept Web (Resources, p. 56), drawing paper, markers

Name ______________________ Date ____________

# KEY SKILL Creating Metaphors

A **metaphor** compares people, objects, and actions that are not alike. However, the two things have characteristics that are the same. In some cases, a writer uses metaphors to explain an idea or thought.

**Examples**

**A.** Dana was a fish when she got in water.
**B.** Ken hammered the ball with the bat.

**Answer the questions.**

**1.** What two things are being compared in Example A? How are these two things alike?

______________________________

______________________________

**2.** What two things are being compared in Example B? How are these two things alike?

______________________________

______________________________

**3.** Do you know another metaphor? Write at least one.

______________________________

______________________________

**For 4–6, follow the directions to write a metaphor. (See Example A.)**

**4.** Name something you do very well.

______________________________

**5.** Name an animal that acts the same way. Explain your choice.

______________________________

**6.** Write a metaphor to show how you are like the animal.

______________________________

Name ______________________ Date ____________

# REFLECT

**Answer the questions.**

**1.** What mascot did you choose for a team?

______________________________________________

**2.** How is this mascot a metaphor for a team playing this sport?

______________________________________________

______________________________________________

**3.** How did naming the characteristics of the sport on the Concept Web help you find a metaphor?

______________________________________________

______________________________________________

**4.** How has choosing the team mascot helped you learn more about the sport?

______________________________________________

______________________________________________

**5.** Do you think that metaphors help explain ideas? Explain.

______________________________________________

______________________________________________

**6.** How will finding metaphors help you think about ways that other things are alike?

______________________________________________

______________________________________________

## Think Link

Think about the special characteristics of your family. Choose a mascot for your family.

Name ______________________________ Date ______________

# After-School Fun

**Lesson 7**

In this lesson, you will work in a group to brainstorm a list of reasons why an after-school sports program would be a good idea for young elementary children. Then, your group will make a simple plan for the program. Finally, you will write a letter to the principal telling him or her about the idea and the details.

## Step 1 — Due Date: ______________

KEY SKILL

**Finding Reasons and Conclusions**

Complete page 24.

## Step 2 — Due Date: ______________

**Think about reasons for the program.**

1. Working in a small group, brainstorm reasons why an after-school sports program would be a good idea for young elementary children. Think of some unusual reasons, too.
2. Get an Ideas Chart. Write a sentence telling about the program in the Topic box.
3. Record the five most important reasons in the numbered boxes on the chart.

## Step 3 — Due Date: ______________

**Plan the program.**

1. Work in your group again. Brainstorm ideas about what the children will do in the program. Will they learn about many different sports or practice skills of sports they know? Will they form teams or stay together in one large group?
2. Write a plan showing what the children will do in the after-school program.

## Step 4 — Due Date: ______________

**Write a letter to the principal.**

1. Review the Ideas Chart and the after-school program plan.
2. Work as a group to write a short letter to the principal telling him or her about the after-school program. Use the reasons you wrote in the Ideas Chart to tell why the program should be considered.

## Step 5 — Due Date: ______________

REFLECT Complete page 25.

**Materials:** Ideas Chart (Resources, p. 57)

Name ______________________ Date ______________

# KEY SKILL Finding Reasons and Conclusions

A **conclusion** is a thought or belief based on **reasons**. When you tell your conclusion and reasons, you are making an **argument** to get another person to think the way you do.

**Example**

Andy says his sister spends too many hours each day playing games on the computer. He says the games keep his sister from exercising. He also says the computer games keep her from thinking creatively.

**Answer the questions.**

**1.** What is Andy's conclusion in the example?

______________________________________________

**2.** What two reasons does Andy give his sister so that she will understand why he thinks the way he does?

______________________________________________

______________________________________________

**3.** Does Andy have good reasons to believe the way he does?

______________________________________________

______________________________________________

**For 4–6, follow the directions to write reasons and a conclusion for an argument.**

**4.** Write what you believe about watching television for several hours each day.

______________________________________________

**5.** Write two reasons that tell why you should or should not watch so much television.

______________________________________________

______________________________________________

**6.** On another sheet of paper, write a paragraph that tells why people should or should not watch several hours of television each day.

Name ______________________ Date ______________

# REFLECT

**Answer the questions.**

1. What did you try to do in your letter to the principal?

_______________________________________________

_______________________________________________

2. What were your reasons for wanting to start an after-school sports program?

_______________________________________________

_______________________________________________

3. How did an Ideas Chart help you organize your thoughts?

_______________________________________________

_______________________________________________

4. How could a chart like this help you share your ideas with others?

_______________________________________________

_______________________________________________

5. How could you use reasons and conclusions to get someone to think the way you do?

_______________________________________________

_______________________________________________

## Think Link

Suppose you want to go to the park. However, your friend wants to go to the movies. What can you tell your friend so that she or he will go with you to the park?

Name ______________________ Date ____________

# Get the Facts

Lesson 8

Sometimes, you might make observations about someone or something when you look at photos. You look at the clues and piece them together to understand what is happening in the photo. However, the answer may be misleading. You have to read the caption to find out what is really taking place. In this lesson, you will learn that you need to get all the facts to understand a situation.

## Step 1

Due Date: ______________________

KEY SKILL

**Inferring**

Complete page 27.

## Step 2

Due Date: ______________________

**Make inferences.**

1. Look through a sports magazine for an interesting picture.
2. Without reading the caption or the article, look at the details of the photo carefully. What do you think is happening?
3. Get a Concept Web. Write a sentence telling what you think is happening in the Topic box.
4. List four inferences you can make about the photo in the large ovals on the web.
5. Write notes about the clues you used to make the inferences in the small ovals.
6. Write your name on a self-stick note. Use it to mark your photo in the magazine.

## Step 3

Due Date: ______________________

**Check your inferences.**

1. Review the inferences you wrote on the Concept Web about the photo.
2. Read the magazine article and the caption for the photo you chose in Step 2.
3. What do you think about the photo now? Do you need to change any of your inferences? If so, circle the inferences that are incorrect. Write new inferences beside the ovals.

## Step 4

Due Date: ______________________

**Write a paragraph.**

1. If you circled an incorrect inference in Step 3, review it. If all of your inferences were correct, look at the photo. Make an incorrect inference about the photo. For example, suppose a baseball player is holding two bats. You could infer that the player wanted to use both bats to make sure he would not miss the ball.
2. Write a paragraph telling a different story about the photo based on an incorrect inference.
3. Share your photo and paragraph with the class.

## Step 5

Due Date: ______________________

REFLECT Complete page 28.

**Materials:** old sports magazines, Concept Web (Resources, p. 56), self-stick notes

Name ______________________ Date ____________

# KEY SKILL Inferring

**Inferring** is using what you know and observe to explain something. You can see something that gives clues. An inference can be right or wrong, so as new information is gathered, an inference can change.

**Example**

As Siti walked toward the football field, she saw the fans sitting on the home team side stand and heard them cheer and clap. She smiled. "The team must have scored a touchdown," Siti thought.

**Answer the questions.**

**1.** In the example, what did Siti think happened?

______________________________

**2.** Tell the clues that helped Siti think this way.

______________________________

**3.** What other information could Siti know from past experience that could help her make this inference?

______________________________

______________________________

**For 4–6, use the picture above to make an inference.**

**4.** Tell what you think happened in the picture.

______________________________

**5.** Tell why you think the way that you do.

______________________________

**6.** List at least three clues that helped you think this way.

______________________________

______________________________

______________________________

Name ______________________ Date ______________

# REFLECT

**Answer the questions.**

**1.** What did you infer about the magazine photo?

______________________________________________

______________________________________________

**2.** What observations helped you make the inference?

______________________________________________

______________________________________________

**3.** Did your inference change when you read the magazine article or caption?

______________________________________________

______________________________________________

**4.** How does observation and known information help you make an inference?

______________________________________________

______________________________________________

**5.** Before making an inference, what should you think about?

______________________________________________

______________________________________________

**6.** How will inferring help you understand other people and things?

______________________________________________

______________________________________________

## Think Link

Have you ever made an inference about someone or a situation and been wrong? Write a paragraph telling what happened.

Name ______________________ Date ____________

# Chore Bore

**Lesson 9**

What chores do you do at home? Which chores do you dislike the most? In this lesson, you will choose the worst chore and invent a machine that will do the job for you.

## Step 1
Due Date: ____________

KEY SKILL

**Solving Problems**

Complete page 30.

## Step 2
Due Date: ____________

**List chores.**

1. Get a Concept Web.
2. Write "Chores" in the Topic box.
3. Brainstorm a list of four chores you dislike doing. Write the names of these chores in the large ovals on your web.
4. Why do you dislike these chores? Write at least two reasons for disliking each chore in the small ovals. Add more ovals if you need to.
5. Which chore do you dislike the most? Circle it.
6. What would happen if you did not do this chore? On the back of the page, list at least four consequences.

## Step 3
Due Date: ____________

**List the steps in a chore.**

1. Think about the chore you dislike the most and the reasons you gave. How do you do it?
2. Get a Sequence Chart. Write the name of the chore you circled on the web as the Title.
3. What materials do you need to do this chore? List them in the oval.
4. Think carefully about each step you do to complete the chore. Write the steps in order in the boxes.

## Step 4
Due Date: ____________

**Invent a machine.**

1. Look at your Sequence Chart to review the steps you listed. What kind of machine could do this job for you? Draw a picture of one machine that could do each step.
2. Explain your invention to the class, telling the steps the machine will do.

## Step 5
Due Date: ____________

REFLECT Complete page 31.

**Materials:** Concept Web (Resources, p. 56), Sequence Chart (Resources, p. 53), drawing paper, crayons

Name ______________________________ Date ______________

# KEY SKILL Solving Problems

When you are **solving a problem**, you are trying to make a situation better. You are trying to find a **solution**. Sometimes you have to make up your mind about a way to solve a problem. You need to look at the choices and think about **consequences**. Consequences are the actions that result from a decision. Consequences can be good or bad.

**Example**

Max needs to feed his dog at night, but he has soccer practice. Then, he is going to a friend's house to spend the night. He was not planning to go home first. What can Max do?

**Answer the questions.**

1. What is the problem in the example?

______________________________________________

2. What are two consequences that might happen if Max does not do this chore?

______________________________________________

______________________________________________

3. What are four solutions to the problem? One of these solutions should be unusual.

______________________________________________

______________________________________________

______________________________________________

______________________________________________

**For 4–7, follow the directions to help Max find a solution to the problem.**

4. Which solution in exercise 3 do you think is the best? Circle it.
5. Write a bad consequence if Max solves the problem this way.

______________________________________________

6. Write a good consequence if Max solves the problem this way.

______________________________________________

7. Do you still think this is the best solution? If not, choose another solution. Think about the good and bad consequences. Write the best solution below.

______________________________________________

Name ______________________ Date ______________

# REFLECT

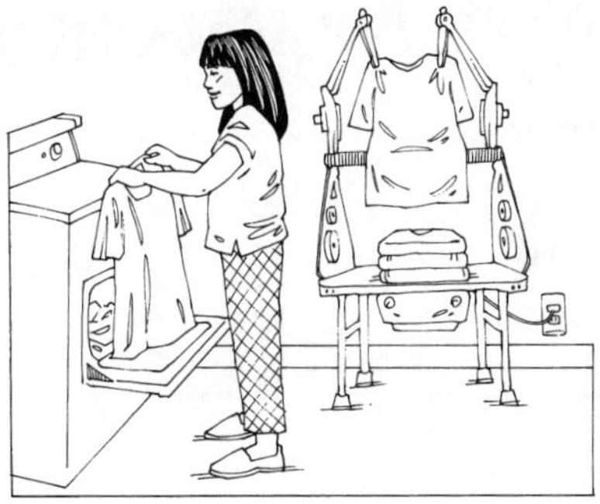

**Answer the questions.**

**1.** What chore do you dislike the most?

______________________________________________

**2.** What is a consequence if the chore is not done?

______________________________________________

______________________________________________

**3.** Why is it important to think about the consequences of an action?

______________________________________________

______________________________________________

**4.** Did thinking about the sequence of steps help you solve the problem? Why or why not?

______________________________________________

______________________________________________

**5.** Sometimes you might have problems with people. How could you use the same process to solve a problem with people?

______________________________________________

______________________________________________

**6.** When you solve another problem, how will you do it next time?

______________________________________________

______________________________________________

## Think Link

Think about a problem you had in school recently. How did you solve the problem? Was there a better way to solve it? Write a paragraph to tell your thoughts.

Name ______________________ Date ______________

# School and Work

Lesson 10

How is going to school like working at an adult's job? In this lesson, you will examine ways they are alike.

## Step 1

Due Date: ______________________

KEY SKILL

**Reasoning by Analogy**

Complete page 33.

## Step 2

Due Date: ______________________

**Write a school schedule.**

1. What do you do most days at school? Write a time schedule of your school activities.
2. At the bottom of the schedule, list activities that the class does on specific days. For example, the class may go to the library each Thursday.

## Step 3

Due Date: ______________________

**Pair school and work activities.**

1. Look at your time schedule. Create a two-column chart. Label one column "School Activities." Label the other "Work Activities."
2. In the School Activities column, list at least ten things you do in school.
3. Work with a partner. Brainstorm how an adult's job is like each listed school activity. For example, if you wrote "work in reading groups," an adult work activity might be "business meeting."
4. If you are unable to think of an analogy between the school and work activities, take the chart home. Ask a family member to help complete the chart.

## Step 4

Due Date: ______________________

**Write a journal entry.**

1. Look at your chart. Write a journal entry that makes one of your school days sound like an adult's day at work.
2. Share your journal entry with the class.

## Step 5

Due Date: ______________________

REFLECT Complete page 34.

Name ______________________ Date ______________

# KEY SKILL Reasoning by Analogy

An **analogy** shows how two items are alike. One item is well known. The other is not as well known. With an analogy, you compare the two items to make learning easier and quicker.

**Example**

Ian was working on a math project. He carefully drew a scale drawing of his bedroom. He labeled all the parts. Then Ian showed his mom the drawing. Ian laughed when he saw his mom drawing blueprints for a house. "Look, Mom, I am an architect, too! I drew a map of the bedroom."

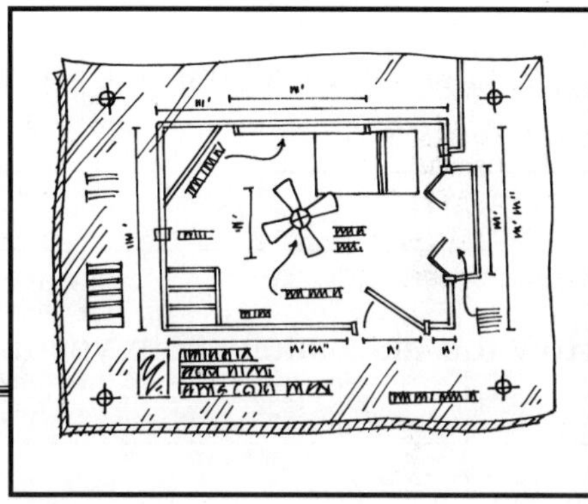

**Answer the questions.**

**1.** What two things are being compared in the example?

______________________________________________

**2.** How are they alike?

______________________________________________

**3.** How does the analogy help you understand what a blueprint is?

______________________________________________

______________________________________________

**For 4–6, follow the directions to write an analogy.**

**4.** Tell what a school cafeteria is used for.

______________________________________________

**5.** Name something that has the same purpose.

______________________________________________

**6.** Write an analogy to tell how the cafeteria is like the item you named above.

______________________________________________

______________________________________________

Name ______________________ Date ______________

# REFLECT

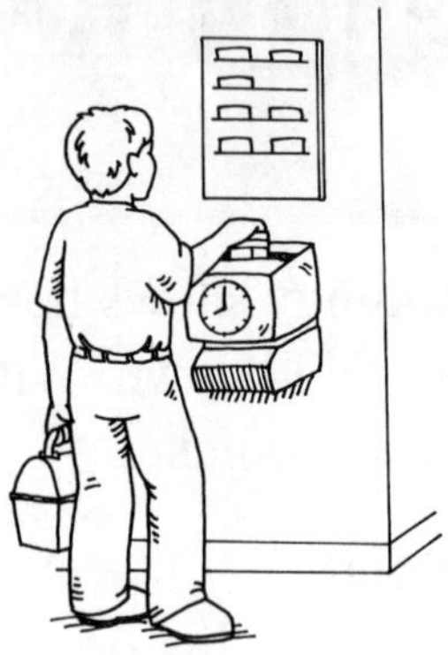

**Answer the questions.**

**1.** How is going to school like working at an adult's job?

______________________________________________

______________________________________________

**2.** How did the analogy help you understand more about the jobs that adults do?

______________________________________________

______________________________________________

**3.** Did a chart help you understand how the two are alike? Explain.

______________________________________________

______________________________________________

**4.** How does showing that two things are alike help you understand the things better?

______________________________________________

______________________________________________

**5.** Is there a better way to learn new information? Explain.

______________________________________________

______________________________________________

## Think Link

How is a family like a small company? Write an analogy.

Name ______________________ Date ____________

# Bake Sale

Lesson 11

Suppose you and a classmate are in charge of planning a bake sale. What kind of cookies will sell the best? You and a partner will take a survey to find the answer and show your data in a graph.

## Step 1
Due Date: ____________

KEY SKILL

**Making Decisions**

Complete page 36.

## Step 2
Due Date: ____________

**Take a survey.**

1. Working with a partner, plan a survey to find out the favorite cookies of the people in the class. What questions will you ask? What kind of people should you ask? How many should you poll to get a big enough sample? How will you record the results?
2. Take the survey and record the results.

## Step 3
Due Date: ____________

**Make a graph.**

1. Review the survey data with your partner. Choose the kind of graph you will use to show the information.
2. Make a graph to show the data.
3. Based on your graph, which cookies should you sell at a bake sale? Circle at least three.
4. Think about consequences of the cookie choices. Could there be any bad consequences of the choices? Some ingredients may be hard to find or too expensive. Make changes in your choices if you need to.
5. Make notes on the graph explaining the choices.

## Step 4
Due Date: ____________

**Draw a bake sale sign.**

1. Review the graph and notes with your partner.
2. Together, make a bake sale sign showing the cookies you will sell.
3. Display your graph and sign.

## Step 5
Due Date: ____________

REFLECT Complete page 37.

**Materials:** drawing paper, crayons

Name ______________________ Date ______________

# KEY SKILL Making Decisions

Sometimes you have to make up your mind about a way to solve a problem. You need to look at the choices and choose the best answer. You are making a **decision**. All decisions have **consequences**. Consequences are the effects of a decision. Consequences can be good or bad.

**Example**

On Saturday, Greg has two chores. He has to clean his room. He also has to collect the trash from all the rooms and take it outside to the trash can. He needs to meet a friend at the library in 30 minutes, so he only has time to get one chore done. Greg wonders what he should do.

**Answer the questions.**

**1.** Look at the example. What is Greg's problem?

______________________

**2.** What are Greg's choices? (Hint: There are more than two choices.)

______________________

______________________

**For 3–6, follow the directions to show a decision Greg might make.**

**3.** Write three facts Greg needs to think about to help him make a decision.

______________________

______________________

______________________

**4.** Circle the most important fact above that will help Greg make the decision.

**5.** Write the choice Greg might make. Explain your choice.

______________________

**6.** Is there a consequence of this choice? If so, write it.

______________________

Name ______________________ Date ____________

# REFLECT

**Answer the questions.**

**1.** Why was taking a poll a good way to decide which cookies to sell at a bake sale?

______________________

______________________

**2.** What facts did you think about that helped you decide which cookies to sell?

______________________

______________________

**3.** Why is it important to think about consequences?

______________________

______________________

**4.** Did thinking about the consequences make you change your cookie choice? Explain.

______________________

______________________

**5.** How can this way of thinking help you make other decisions?

______________________

______________________

**6.** When is it a good idea to ask other people for help in making a decision?

______________________

______________________

## Think Link

How should you decide what price to sell the cookies for at the bake sale? What do you need to think about when making this decision? What are some consequences of your decision? Work with your partner to decide prices of cookies. Write the prices on the bake sale sign.

Name ______________________ Date ______________

# Baby-Sitting Safety

Lesson 12

Baby-sitting is a job many students do, either for brothers and sisters or for other families in the neighborhood. It is a big responsibility, though. In this lesson, you will identify possible harmful situations and think about what could happen to small children.

## Step 1 Due Date: ______________

KEY SKILL

### Determining Cause and Effect

Complete page 39.

## Step 2 Due Date: ______________

**Identify inside harmful situations.**

1. Get the Safe or Not Safe sheet.
2. Circle all the pictures that show unsafe situations.
3. Get a Cause and Effect Charts sheet. Write a description of each unsafe action in a Cause box. Write an effect in the Effect box.
4. With a partner, talk about each cause and effect you wrote. Discuss what a baby-sitter can do to prevent accidents.

## Step 3 Due Date: ______________

**Identify outside harmful situations.**

1. Get a Cause and Effect Charts sheet.
2. Working with a partner, brainstorm a list of harmful situations that might happen outside. Write each idea in a Cause box. Write an effect in the Effect box.
3. Together, discuss what a baby-sitter can do to prevent accidents outside. Also, discuss the importance of knowing emergency numbers.

## Step 4 Due Date: ______________

**Make a list of baby-sitting rules.**

1. Review the Cause and Effect sheets listing harmful situations.
2. Make a list of rules that would help keep children safe.
3. Share your rules with the class.
4. Compile all of the rules to make a baby-sitter handbook.

## Step 5 Due Date: ______________

REFLECT Complete page 40.

**Materials:** Safe or Not Safe? (Resources, p. 63), Cause and Effect Charts (Resources, p. 58)

Name ______________________ Date ______________

# KEY SKILL Determining Cause and Effect

A **cause** is the reason something happens. An **effect** is what happens.

**Example**

Ron was baby-sitting his baby sister, Lena. Lena giggled every time Ron shook the rattle near her. All of a sudden, Lena began to cry. Ron looked at the clock. He realized Lena was probably hungry. He picked her up and walked to the kitchen.

**Answer the questions.**

**1.** What is a cause in the example?

______________________________________________

**2.** What is an effect in the example?

______________________________________________

**3.** What is the cause and effect in the following sentence?
Lena drank the milk quickly after Ron heated it in a pan of hot water.

| Cause | Effect |
| --- | --- |
| ______________ | ______________ |

**For 4–5, complete each sentence. Tell if you wrote a "cause" or an "effect."**

**4.** When Lena was finished, she ______________________________

______________________________________________

**5.** Lena's eyes began to close, so Ron ______________________________

______________________________________________

Name ______________________ Date ______________

# REFLECT

**Answer the questions.**

**1.** Do you think baby-sitting is an easy job? Explain.

______________________________________________

______________________________________________

**2.** How can thinking about causes and effects help you be a better baby-sitter?

______________________________________________

______________________________________________

**3.** Did using the Cause and Effect Charts help you think about harmful baby-sitting situations? Explain.

______________________________________________

______________________________________________

**4.** How can you use cause and effect to help you prevent problems before they happen?

______________________________________________

______________________________________________

**5.** How can you use cause and effect to help you to think before you act?

______________________________________________

______________________________________________

## Think Link

Suppose a small child is crying. What could be the cause? List as many causes as you can.

Name ______________________________ Date ______________

# Game Time

Lesson 13

There are many things to do at a carnival, including rides, food, and games. But how much money do you spend trying to win the biggest stuffed animal? You and a partner will list and examine important factors that determine how challenging some carnival games are. After thinking about questions to ask and observations to make, you will plan a fair game for a school carnival.

## Step 1 Due Date: ______________

KEY SKILL **Uncovering Assumptions**

Complete page 42.

## Step 2 Due Date: ______________

**List carnival games.**

1. Get a Concept Web. Write "Carnival Games" in the Topic box.
2. Working with a partner, brainstorm a list of carnival games. Write the names or descriptions of four of your favorite games in the large ovals.
3. Write at least two reasons each game is a challenge in the small ovals. Draw more ovals if needed.

## Step 3 Due Date: ______________

**Uncover game assumptions.**

1. With your partner, review the Concept Web. Think about whether it would be better to ask the game operator about the game or observe other people as they play the game.
2. Beside each small oval, write a question you could ask or an observation you could make to learn more about the game to uncover assumptions.
3. Which game do you think is the most challenging to win? Circle it.

## Step 4 Due Date: ______________

**Design a carnival game.**

1. Think about the game that you circled on the web. Suppose your school is having a carnival. How can you make a similar game that will be fair? Will you need to make different rules? Think about changes you can make to the carnival game to make it fair.
2. Draw a picture of the game. Write a description of the game and its rules.
3. Share the drawing and the game rules with the class.

## Step 5 Due Date: ______________

REFLECT Complete page 43.

**Materials:** Concept Web (Resources, p. 56), drawing paper, crayons

Name ______________________ Date ______________

# KEY SKILL Uncovering Assumptions

When you believe that something is true without knowing all the facts, you are making an **assumption**. It is important to check the facts before believing the information. You need to **uncover assumptions** so that you will make the right choices.

**Example**
Won-He saw an ad in a magazine for a new computer game. The ad said only the very best could get through the different game levels. Won-He thought the game would be a great challenge since he was such a whiz on a computer. He decided to go buy the game.

**Answer the questions.**

**1.** Why does Won-He want to buy the computer game?

______________________________________________

**2.** What does Won-He assume about the game after reading the ad in a magazine?

______________________________________________

______________________________________________

**3.** Should Won-He believe the ad? Explain.

______________________________________________

______________________________________________

**For 4–5, follow the directions to help Won-He uncover an assumption.**

**4.** Write two questions Won-He should ask himself about the magazine ad.

______________________________________________

______________________________________________

**5.** Tell how Won-He can discover if the computer game will be as challenging as the ad says.

______________________________________________

______________________________________________

Name ______________________ Date ____________

# REFLECT

**Answer the questions.**

**1.** Do you think carnival games are fair or unfair? Explain.

______________________________________________

**2.** What do you need to think about before playing a carnival game?

______________________________________________

______________________________________________

**3.** Is it a good idea to write a list of questions to ask or observations to make before playing a game? Explain.

______________________________________________

______________________________________________

**4.** Why is it good to uncover assumptions?

______________________________________________

______________________________________________

**5.** How will uncovering assumptions help you make choices?

______________________________________________

______________________________________________

## Think Link

Think about a product ad you saw on television that made you want to buy it. What assumptions did you make about the product? Write a list of questions to uncover some assumptions about it.

Name ______________________________ Date ______________

# Town Tour

Lesson 14

Suppose a friend is coming to visit and wants to take a tour of special places in your town. What places do you think your friend will want to see? Plan an all-day tour of interesting and special places to visit in your town.

## Step 1

Due Date: ______________________

KEY SKILL

**Determining Reliability of Sources**

Complete page 45.

## Step 2

Due Date: ______________________

**Begin a KWHL Chart about tourist sights.**

1. Get a KWHL Chart. In the "K" column, make a list of tourist sights in your area.
2. Are there facts you need to discover about the places you listed in the "K" column? Should you research information to find out if there are other places your friend should visit? Write what you want to know in the "W" column.
3. Write how you plan to find the information about your town in the "H" column. List five different sources. Don't forget about people to whom you can talk.

## Step 3

Due Date: ______________________

**Complete the KWHL Chart.**

1. Look at the "H" column of your KWHL Chart. Are all the sources reliable? Circle the three best sources where you could find information about your town.
2. Research the sources you circled in the KWHL Chart. Tell your teacher if you need extra time to talk with someone.
3. Write the information you find in the "L" column of the KWHL Chart.

## Step 4

Due Date: ______________________

**Plan the tour.**

1. Choose the best places to visit in your town. Think about in what order you will visit these places and how long you will need to stay.
2. Make a travel brochure showing the all-day tour you and your friend will take. Draw pictures of the places you will visit in the order you will travel. Be sure to include a place to eat lunch!
3. Under each picture, write the time schedule.

## Step 5

Due Date: ______________________

REFLECT Complete page 46.

**Materials:** KWHL Chart (Resources, p. 59), resources for tourist sights, drawing paper, crayons

Name ______________________ Date ______________

# KEY SKILL Determining Reliability of Sources

**Sources** are the places you go to find information. People, books, magazines, newspapers, and the Internet can be sources. The sources need to be **reliable**. You have to be able to trust that the information is true.

**Example**

Wes wrote a list of sources where he might find information about good restaurants in his town.

**A.** *A Diner's Guide*, a book written by John Thomas in 1965

**B.** Talk with Raz Berry, a chef

**C.** Talk with my little brother

**D.** Look for restaurant reviews in the newspaper

**E.** Look up the subject "restaurants" in an up-to-date telephone book

**Answer the questions.**

**1.** Which sources in the example would provide useful information?

______________________________________

**2.** Which sources in the example would not be useful? Explain.

______________________________________

______________________________________

**For 3–5, follow the directions to list sources that would be reliable.**

**3.** Think about a town's history. Name two kinds of books where you could find information.

______________________________________

______________________________________

**4.** Name two people who could give you good information about a town's history.

______________________________________

**5.** List some key words you could type on the Internet to find information about a town's history.

______________________________________

Name ______________________ Date ______________

# REFLECT

Answer the questions.

**1.** What were some reliable sources you used to find information about places to visit?

______________________________________________

______________________________________________

**2.** Why might a travel brochure published many years ago not be a reliable source?

______________________________________________

______________________________________________

**3.** How could you decide if a person is a reliable source of information?

______________________________________________

______________________________________________

**4.** What might happen if a source you choose is not reliable?

______________________________________________

______________________________________________

**5.** When might you need to think about reliable sources for school projects and activities?

______________________________________________

______________________________________________

## Think Link

Suppose you want to get directions to a museum. What reliable sources could you use?

Name ______________________ Date ______________

# Make A Game

Lesson 15

Have you ever said, "I'm bored! There's nothing to do"? Well, here is a way to prevent future boredom. Work with a partner to brainstorm a new game!

## Step 1
Due Date: ______________________

KEY SKILL **Generating Possibilities**

Complete page 48.

## Step 2
Due Date: ______________________

**List ideas.**

1. Work with a partner. Get a Concept Web.
2. Write "New Game" in the Topic box.
3. Brainstorm four ways to move a tennis ball. Try to include at least one unusual idea. Record them on the chart in the large ovals.
4. In the small ovals, write notes about how to use two tennis balls and a jump rope to make a new game using the motion in the large ovals.

## Step 3
Due Date: ______________________

**Write game rules.**

1. Review the Concept Web with your partner. Choose one idea for a new game. Circle it.
2. Write the rules for a new game. Think about the object of the game, how many people can play, where it should be played, and the rules.
3. Play the game with your partner. Does it make sense? Improve the game if needed.

## Step 4
Due Date: ______________________

**Teach the game.**

With your partner, teach the game to the class.

## Step 5
Due Date: ______________________

REFLECT Complete page 49.

**Materials:** Concept Web (Resources, p. 56), two tennis balls, jump rope

Name ______________________ Date ____________

# KEY SKILL Generating Possibilities

Some problems are difficult to solve. At times there may be many solutions. At other times there may only be one way. It is important to **generate possibilities** when solving any problem. This means listing all the ways to solve the problem—even if the ideas are different and unusual.

**Example**

Tara is invited to a friend's house, but Tara's mother is unable to take her. What can Tara do?

**A.** Ask her friend's mother to come get her
**B.** Walk
**C.** Ride a bike
**D.** Ride in a wagon
**E.** Not go

### Answer the questions.

**1.** What is the problem in the example?

______________________________________________

**2.** Which idea is unusual? Write the letter of the answer. ____________

**3.** What other ideas might Tara think about? Name three.

______________________________________________

______________________________________________

______________________________________________

### For 4–5, follow the directions to generate possibilities.

**4.** Tara is in a school play, and she was asked to bring props. She left the list at school. What can she do? Name three ideas.

______________________________________________

______________________________________________

______________________________________________

**5.** Name an unusual way for Tara to solve her problem.

______________________________________________

______________________________________________

Name ____________________ Date ____________

# REFLECT

**Answer the questions.**

**1.** What helped you and your partner think of ways to use the balls and rope?

______________________________________________

______________________________________________

**2.** How did using the Concept Web help you think of ideas?

______________________________________________

______________________________________________

**3.** How did you choose the best idea?

______________________________________________

______________________________________________

**4.** Why do you think it is important to generate possibilities before making a decision?

______________________________________________

______________________________________________

**5.** How can this way of thinking help you make other decisions?

______________________________________________

______________________________________________

## Think Link

Pencils are useful tools until the eraser is gone. Then, they are generally thrown away. Think of ways to recycle a pencil without an eraser. Be sure to include some unusual ideas, too.

Name ____________________ Date ____________

# Tic-Tac-Toe Moves

**Lesson 16**

In many board games, you need to think about the moves that you will make in order to win as well as to block another player's moves. It is important to think ahead and to predict what your opponent will do. In this lesson, you will play tic-tac-toe to determine your game-playing skills.

## Step 1

Due Date: ____________________

KEY SKILL

**Predicting**

Complete page 51.

## Step 2

Due Date: ____________________

**Play tic-tac-toe to make generalizations.**

1. Work with a partner. Each of you should draw several tic-tac-toe boards.
2. Play at least four games. As you move, try to think ahead. Think to yourself, *If I write an* O *in this square, where might the other player write an* X*? What move will I be able to make afterwards?*
3. Each partner should get an Ideas Chart. Work alone to list at least five generalizations you can make about strategies for playing tic-tac-toe.
4. Discuss the generalizations with your partner.

## Step 3

Due Date: ____________________

**Play tic-tac-toe to make predictions.**

1. Work with a different partner than you did in Step 2. Each of you should draw several tic-tac-toe boards.
2. Review the generalizations you wrote on the Ideas Chart.
3. Play at least four games. Think ahead and try to predict where your partner will move. Are your generalizations still true?
4. Did one of you win more games than the other? If so, why? Discuss your findings.

## Step 4

Due Date: ____________________

**Play a tic-tac-toe tournament.**

1. Organize the class to play a tic-tac-toe tournament. Play ten games with different classmates. Record your wins and losses on a chart.
2. Have the top players share their strategies for playing tic-tac-toe.

## Step 5

Due Date: ____________________

REFLECT Complete page 52.

**Materials:** Ideas Chart (Resources, p. 57)

Name ______________________ Date ______________

# KEY SKILL Predicting

**Predicting** is telling what will happen next. To make a prediction, think about what you know. Also, look for clues in pictures you see and resources you read. As you learn more facts, you may have to change your prediction.

**Example**

Erin and Tony were in the park. They watched gray clouds blow in from the north. The clouds gathered overhead and covered the sun. A spark of lightning flashed overhead, followed by a crack of thunder. Erin and Tony began to look for a safe place out of the storm.

**Answer the questions.**

**1.** What do you think will happen next in the example?

______________________

**2.** What makes you think this way?

______________________

______________________

**For 3–5, follow the directions to make a prediction about the weather.**

**3.** Tell what weather condition will happen next.

______________________

**4.** List the clues that helped you make this prediction.

______________________

**5.** Tell how knowing about storms helped you predict what would happen next.

______________________

______________________

Name ______________________________ Date ______________

# REFLECT

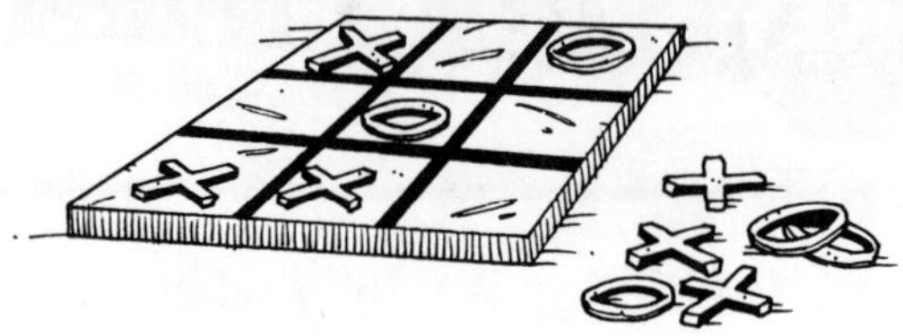

**Answer the questions.**

**1.** How did thinking ahead help you play tic-tac-toe?

___________________________________________________________

**2.** Were you able to predict the other player's moves? Explain.

___________________________________________________________

___________________________________________________________

**3.** How did making generalizations help you predict moves?

___________________________________________________________

___________________________________________________________

**4.** Did playing more games with many different players improve your predicting skills?

___________________________________________________________

___________________________________________________________

**5.** How can predicting help you make choices?

___________________________________________________________

___________________________________________________________

## Think Link

Checkers is another board game where predicting moves in advance can be important to winning. Play several games of checkers with a classmate. Make some generalizations about different moves. Play several more games. Did you win more often?

Name ______________________ Date ______________

# Sequence Chart

**Title:** ______________________

Name ______________________ Date ____________

# Venn Diagram

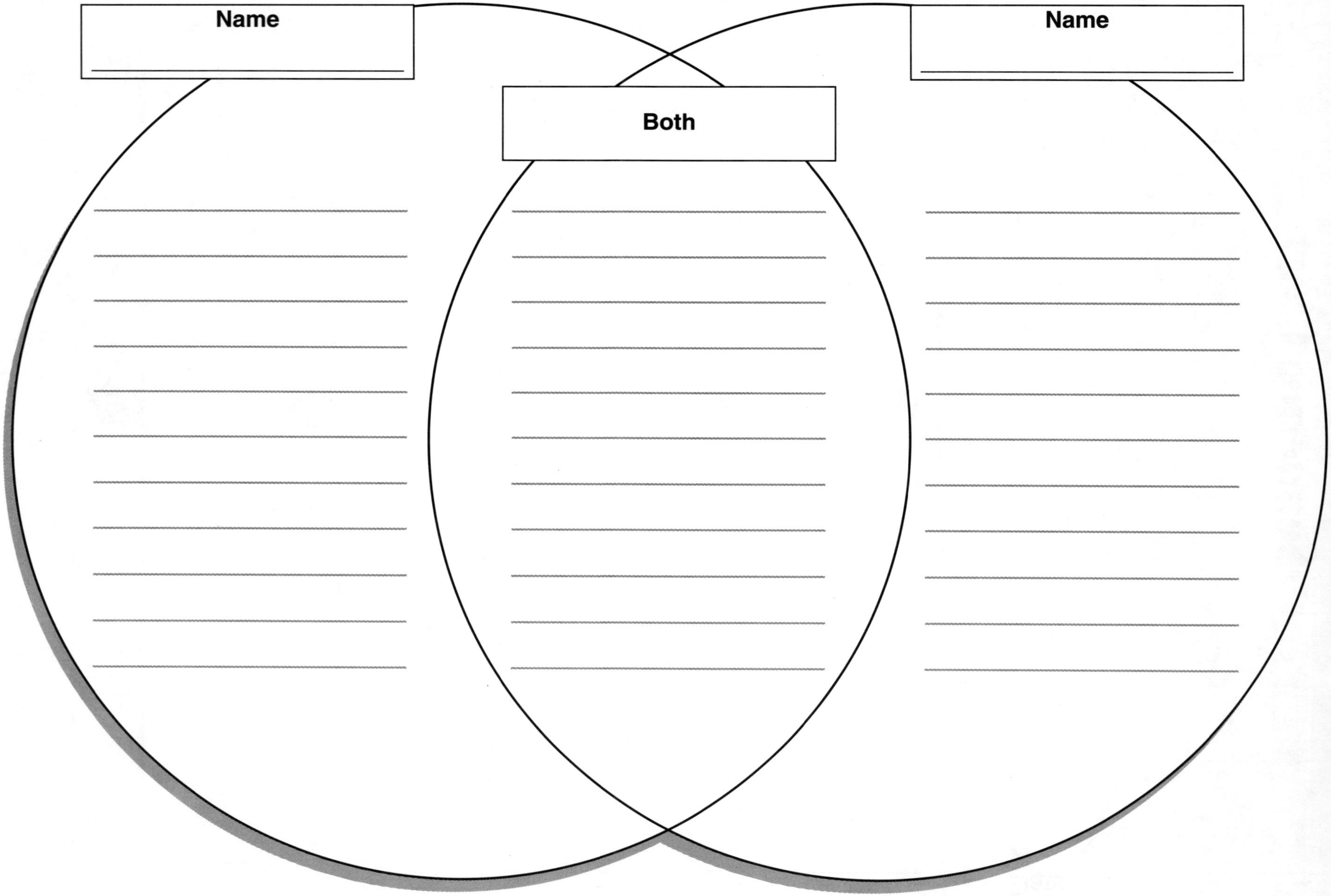

Name ______________________ Date ______________

# Matrix Chart

| | Landforms to Compare | | | |
|---|---|---|---|---|
| **Resources** | | | | |
| | | | | |
| | | | | |
| | | | | |
| | | | | |
| | | | | |
| | | | | |
| | | | | |
| | | | | |

Name ____________________ Date __________

# Concept Web

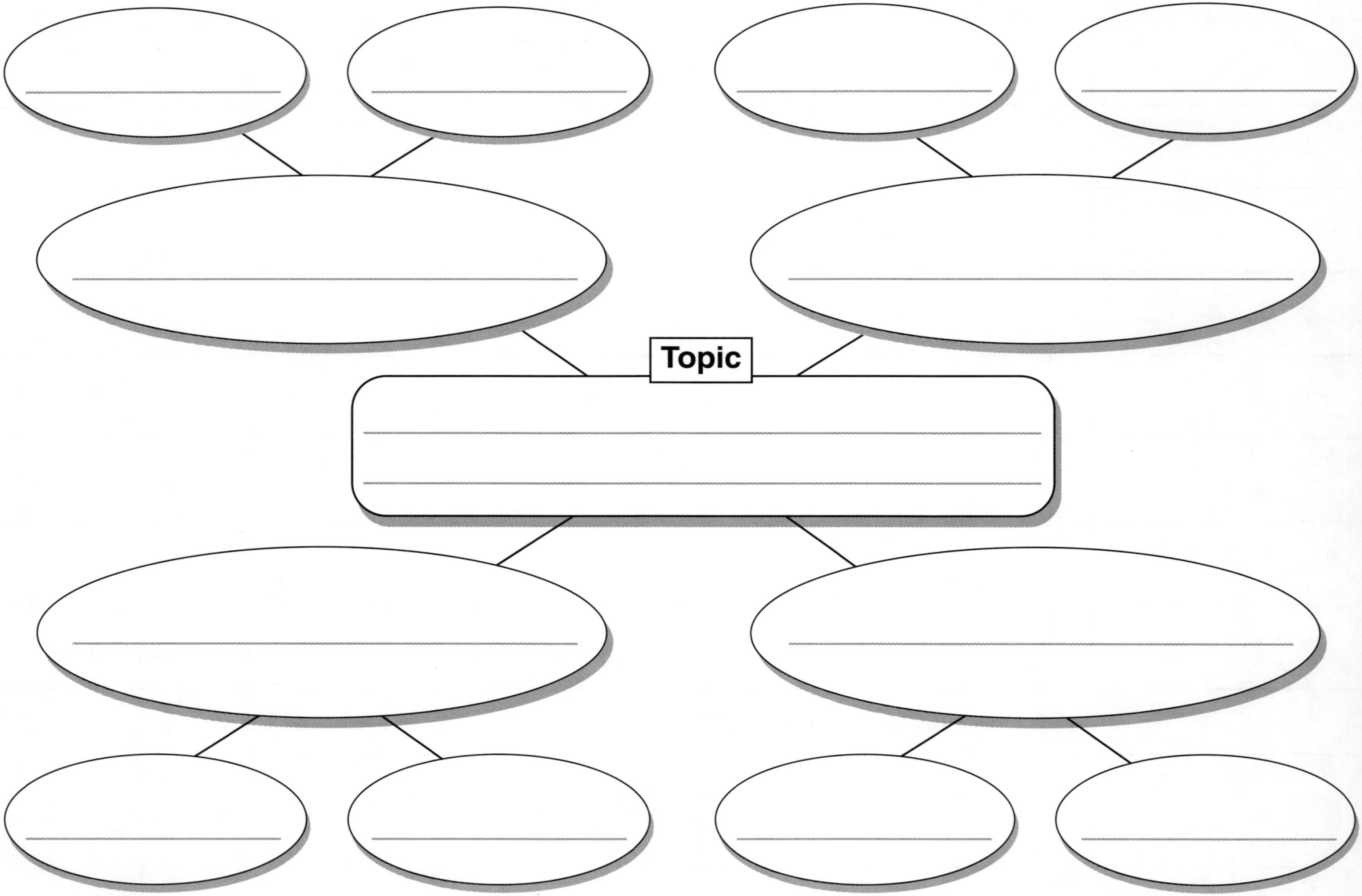

Name ______________________ Date ______________

# Ideas Chart

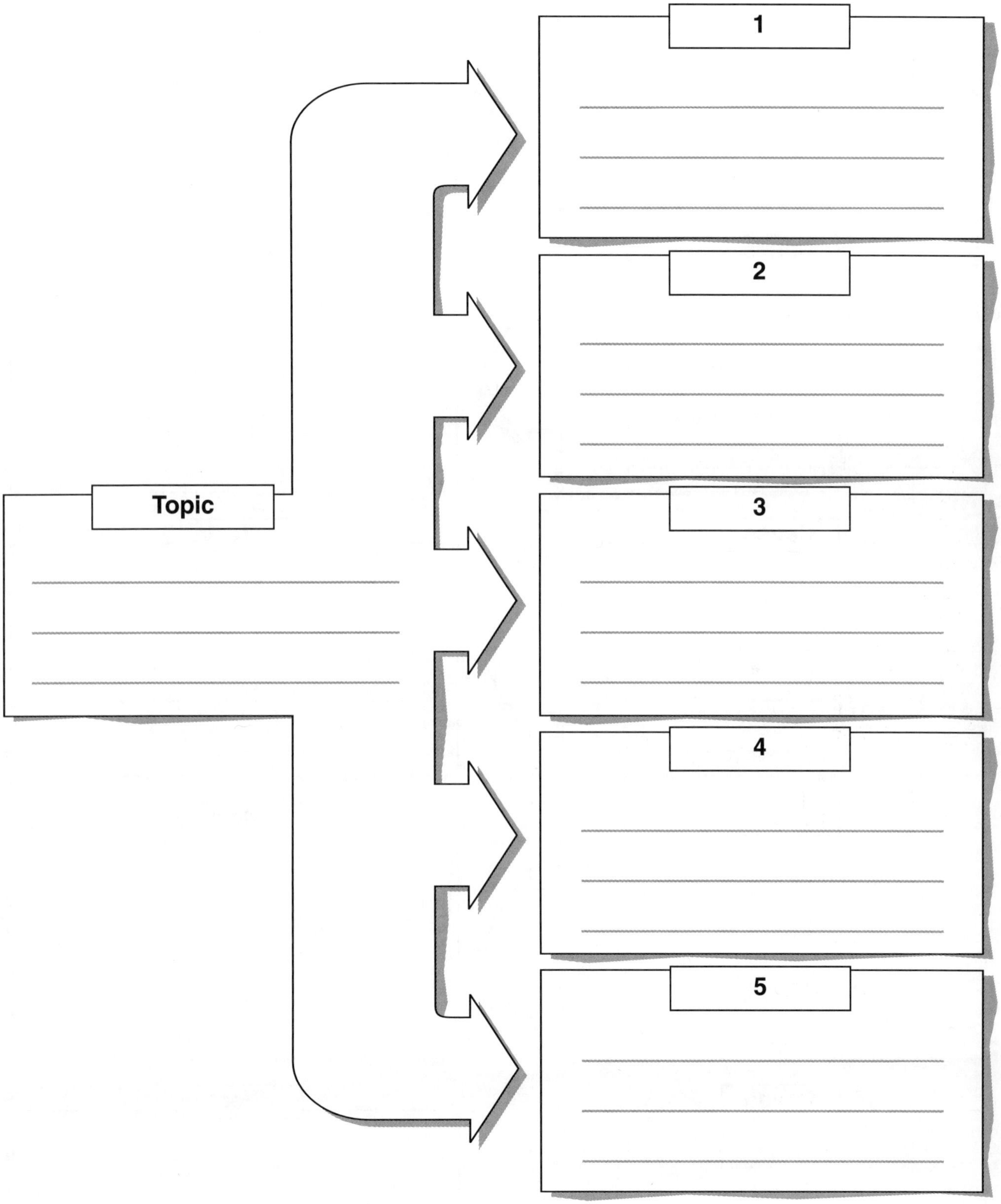

Name ______________________ Date ______________

# Cause and Effect Charts

| Cause | Effect |
| --- | --- |
| | |

| Cause | Effect |
| --- | --- |
| | |

| Cause | Effect |
| --- | --- |
| | |

| Cause | Effect |
| --- | --- |
| | |

| Cause | Effect |
| --- | --- |
| | |

Name ______________________ Date ______________

# KWHL Chart

| K<br>What do I **KNOW**? | W<br>What do I **WANT** to know? | H<br>**HOW** will I learn? | L<br>What did I **LEARN**? |
| --- | --- | --- | --- |
| | | | |
| | | | |
| | | | |
| | | | |
| | | | |
| | | | |
| | | | |
| | | | |
| | | | |
| | | | |
| | | | |
| | | | |
| | | | |
| | | | |

Name ________________________________ Date ________________

# Graph Paper

Name ______________________ Date ______________

# Bend River Map

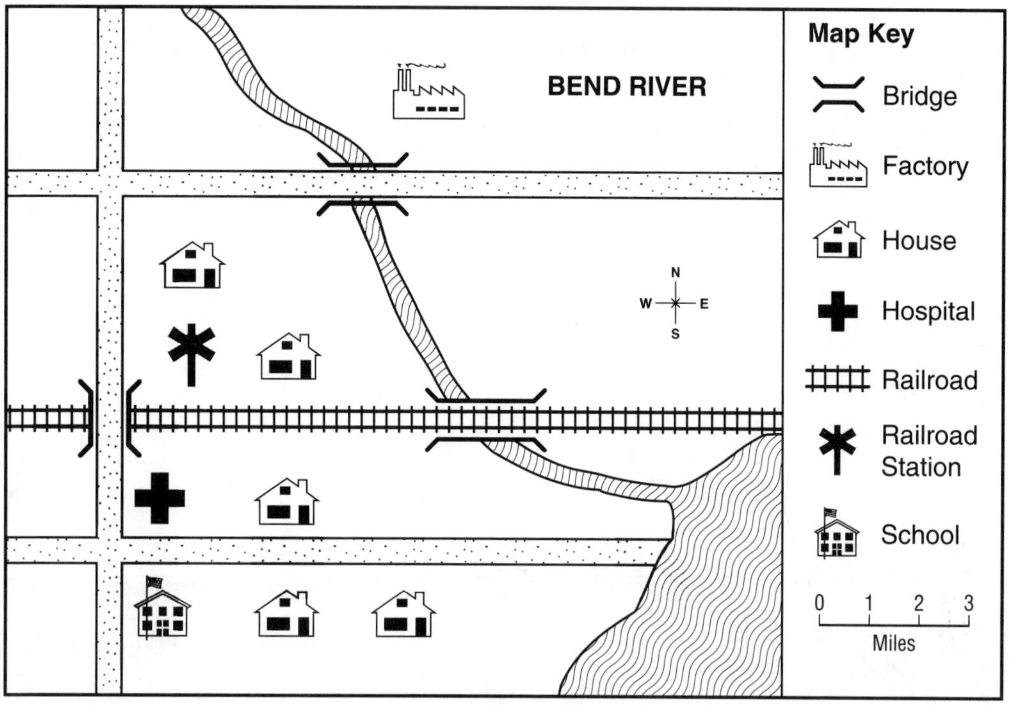


# Brazil Maps

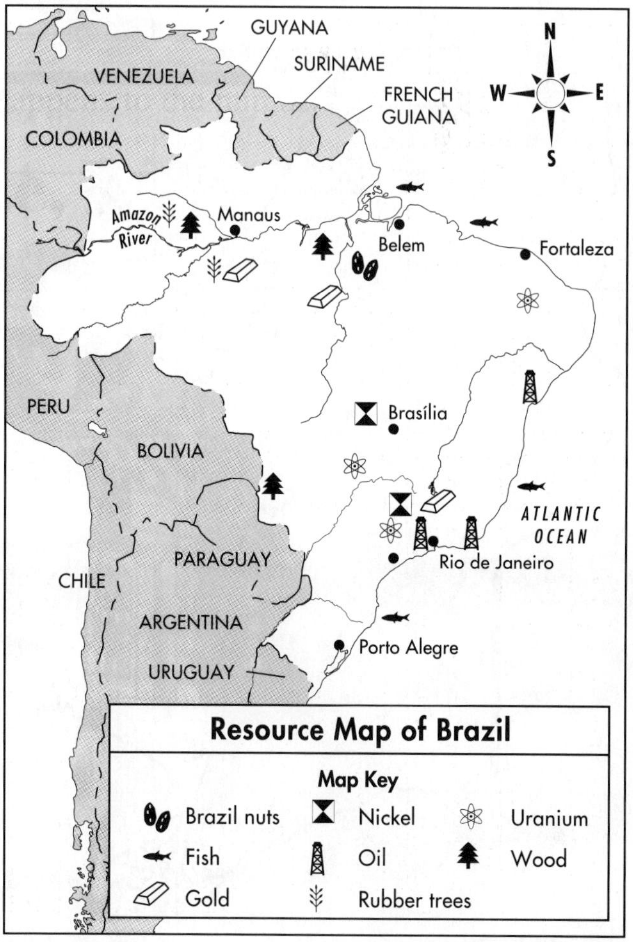

Name ______________________ Date ______________

# Map of Asouby

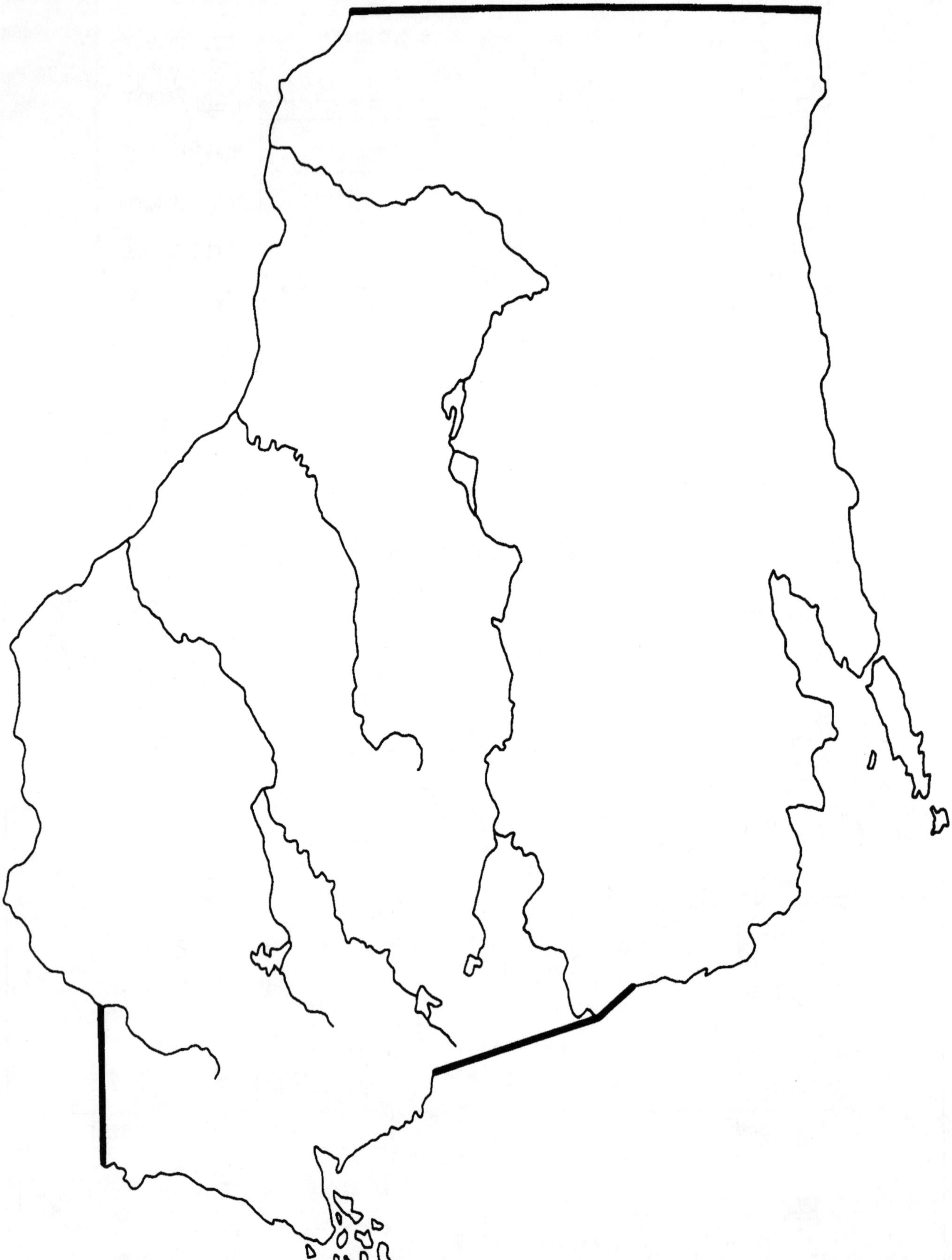

Name ____________________ Date ____________

# Safe or Not Safe?

**1.**

**2.**

**3.**

**4.**

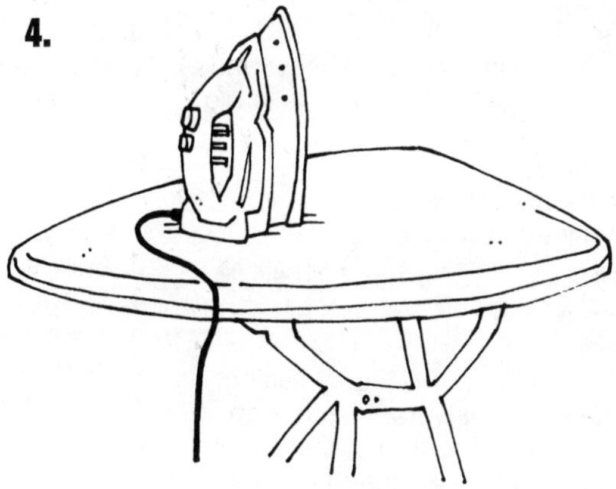

**5.**

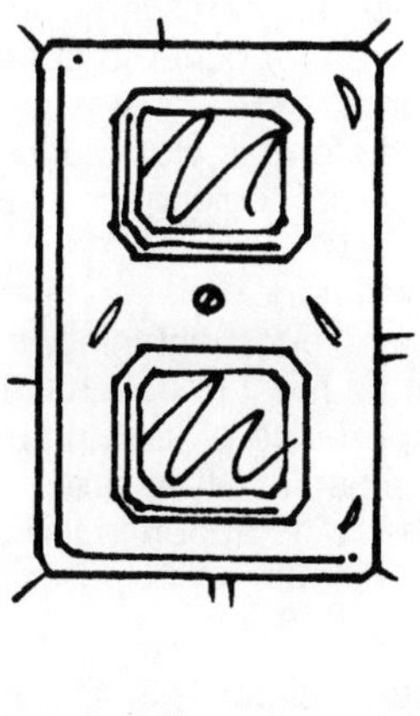

______________________

**6.**

______________________

# Thinking Skills: Grade 6

## Answer Key

**p. 6**
1. a title and distance scale
2. a map
3. Fred does not know how far he needs to drive.
4. Answers will vary.
5. Answers will vary.
6. Answers will vary.

**p. 9**
1. walks her dog
2. north
3. southeast
4. 7 blocks
5. Possible answer: a pencil and a sharpener
6. Possible answer: First, put the pencil in the hole of the sharpener. Then, turn the handle of the sharpener in a clockwise movement seven times. Next, check your pencil. Repeat the process until the pencil is sharp.

**p. 12**
1. Austin and Houston
2. They are cities.; They are in Texas.
3. Houston is in the southeast and is a shipping city. Austin is in the center and is the capital.
4. Answers will vary.
5. Answers will vary.
6. Answers will vary.

**p. 15**
1. the ocean
2. fish
3. They earned a living by fishing.
4. Possible answers: Fish are an important resource of the ocean. People who live near the ocean may earn a living by fishing.
5. Possible answer: Most cities in Brazil are located beside bodies of water.
6. Answers will vary.

**p. 18**
1. sizes of balls
2. how the ball is moved
3. Answers will vary.
4. Answers will vary.
5. Answers will vary.

**p. 21**
1. A girl who swims very well is being compared with a fish.
2. Hitting a ball is compared to the way a hammer swings.
3. Answers will vary.
4. Answers will vary.
5. Answers will vary.
6. Answers will vary.

**p. 24**
1. Playing games on the computer for many hours is not good for his sister.
2. Playing computer games keeps his sister from getting exercise and thinking creatively.
3. Most likely answer: Yes, there are many resources that say this is true.
4. Answers will vary.
5. Answers will vary.
6. Answers will vary.

**p. 27**
1. The home team scored a touchdown.
2. The fans stood, cheered, and clapped.
3. Possible answer: Most teams stand, cheer, and clap when a team scores or makes an important play.
4. Answers will vary.
5. Answers will vary.
6. Answers will vary.

**p. 30**
1. Max needs to feed his dog, but he has other activities he wants to do.
2. Possible answers: The dog will be hungry., His mother will be angry.
3. Answers will vary.
4. Answers will vary.
5. Answers will vary.
6. Answers will vary.
7. Answers will vary.

**p. 33**
1. a scale drawing of a bedroom with the blueprints of a house
2. They are drawings of places.
3. A blueprint is like a map. It shows what a house looks like.
4. It is a place where students eat.
5. Possible answer: a restaurant
6. Answers will vary.

**p. 36**
1. Greg can only get one chore done before he has to leave.
2. Greg can do one chore before he leaves and the other one when he gets back. Greg can do both chores very quickly before he leaves. Greg can call his friend and change the meeting time. Greg can ask his brother or sister to help him do his chores quickly.
3. Answers will vary.
4. Answers will vary.
5. Answers will vary.
6. Answers will vary.

**p. 39**
1. Possible answers: Ron shook the rattle or Lena is hungry.
2. Possible answers: Lena giggled or Lena cries.
3. Cause: Ron warms a bottle of milk. Effect: Lena drinks the milk.
4. Answers will vary.
5. Answers will vary.

**p. 42**
1. The ad makes the computer game look interesting.
2. that it will be challenging
3. Answers will vary.
4. Answers will vary.
5. Answers will vary.

**p. 45**
1. B, D
2. Source A is too old.; Source C most likely does not have facts about the topic, only opinions.; Source E would only give addresses, phone numbers, and advertisements, not recommendations.
3. Answers will vary.
4. Answers should reflect people who have a job associated with the town, lived in the town for a long time, or work for a travel company.
5. Answers should reflect words and phrases that have to do with history and a town's name.

**p. 48**
1. Tara wants to go to a friend's house, but her mom cannot take her.
2. D
3. Answers will vary.
4. Answers will vary.
5. Answers will vary.

**p. 51**
1. Most likely answer: Erin and Tony will run for cover to get out of the storm.
2. The storm is close, and Erin and Tony are looking for a safe place to stay.
3. It will rain.
4. gray clouds, lightning, thunder
5. Since most people have the experience of seeing and hearing a rainstorm, they are prepared for what will happen in the same conditions.

**p. 63**
Students circle 1, 3, 4, and 6.